The World in a Supermarket

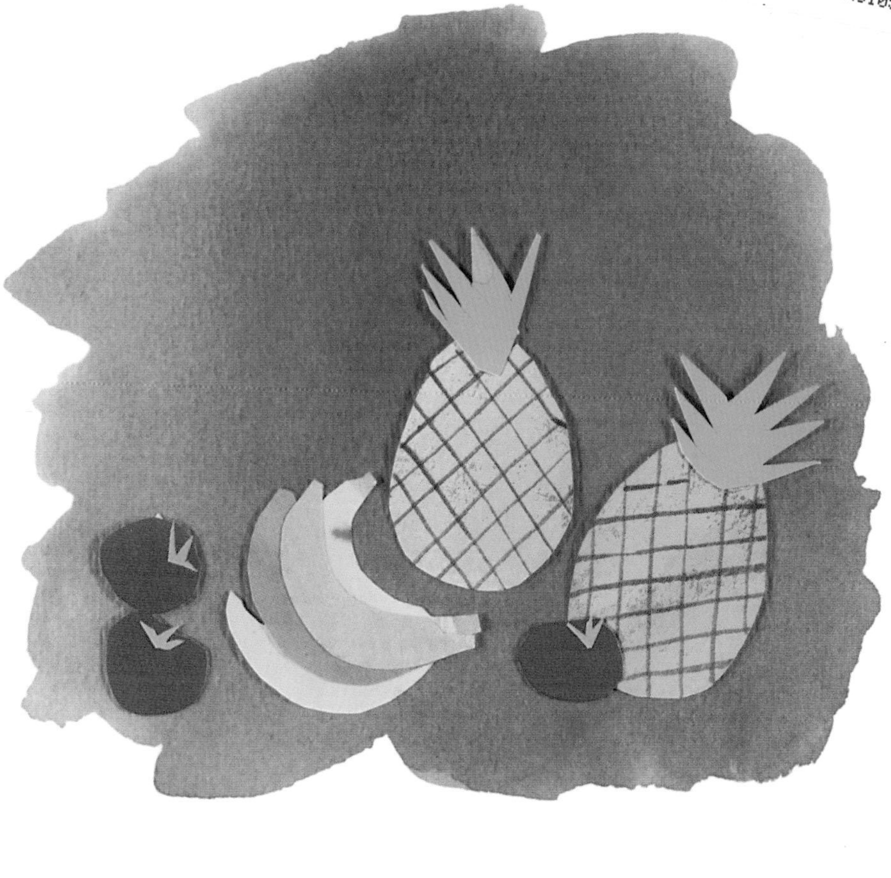

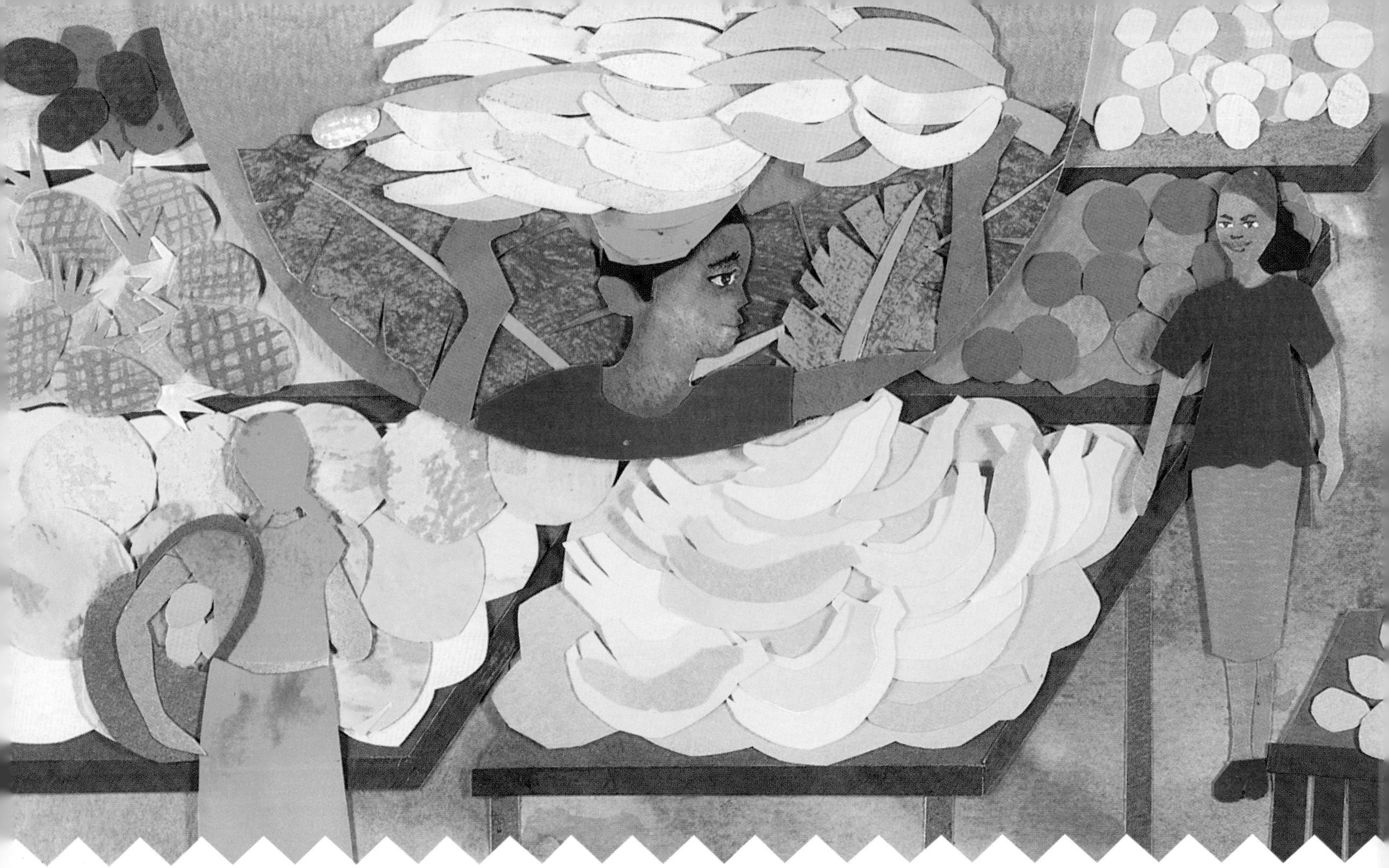

Bananas from Honduras.

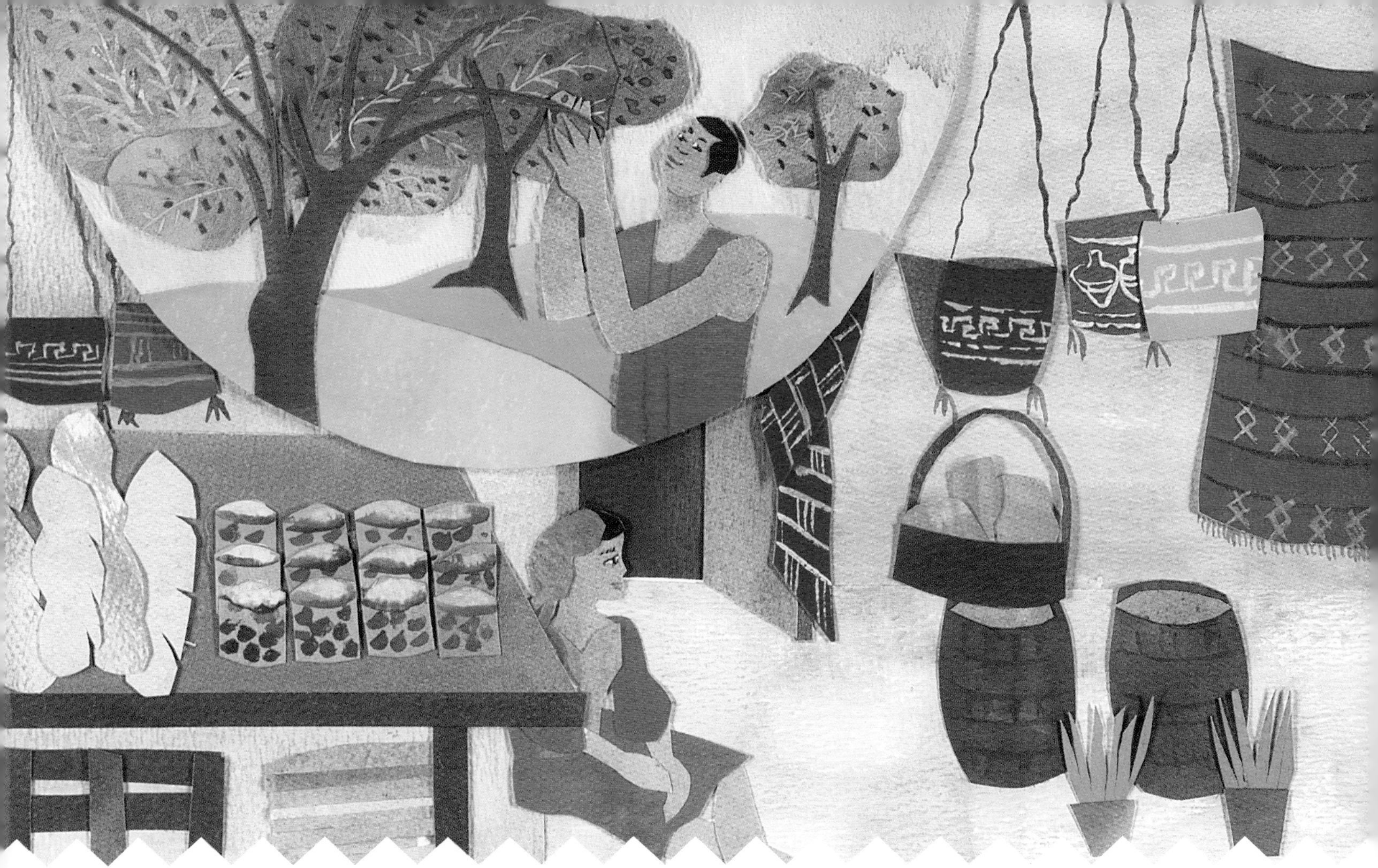

Olives from Greece.

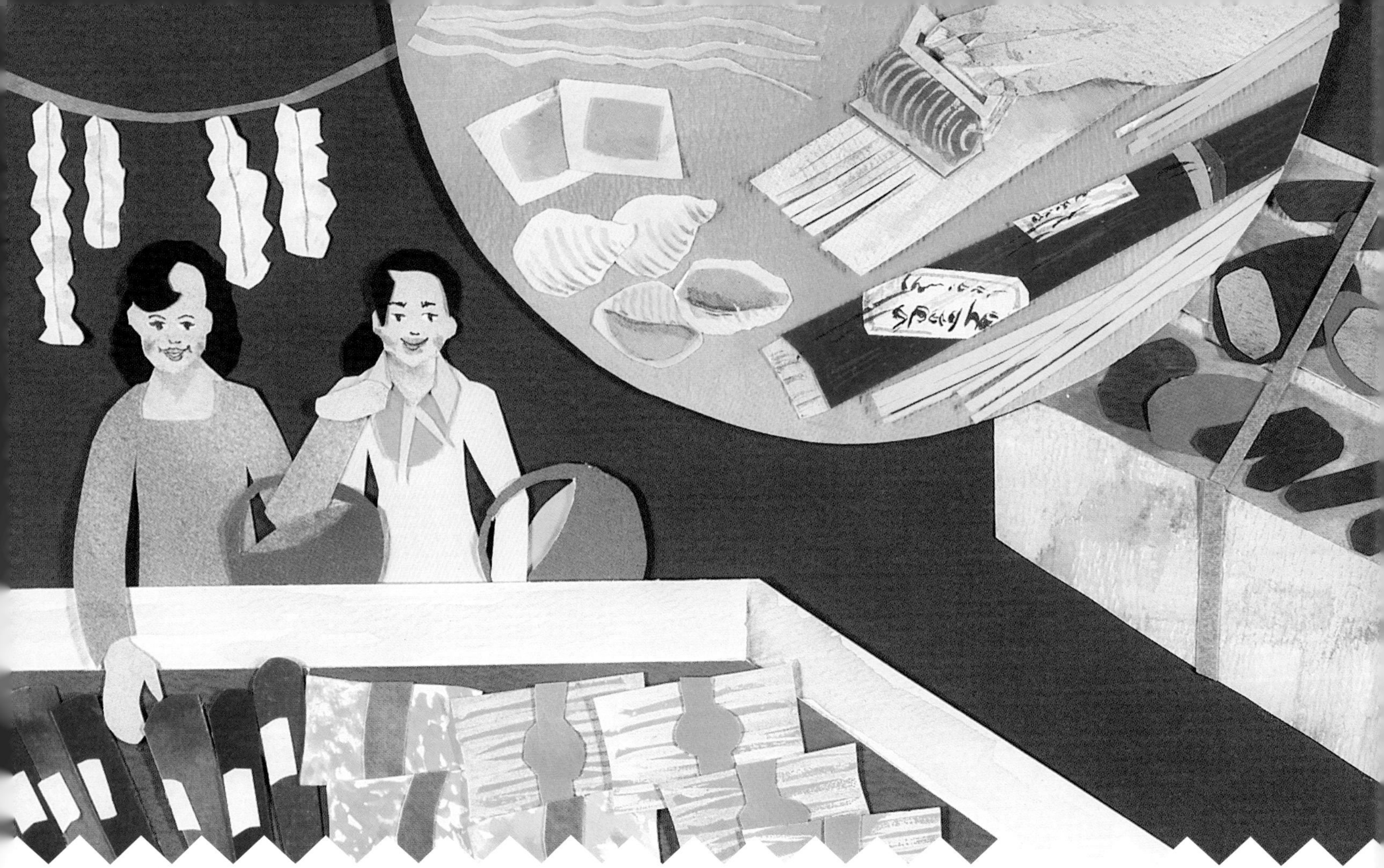

Pasta from Italy.

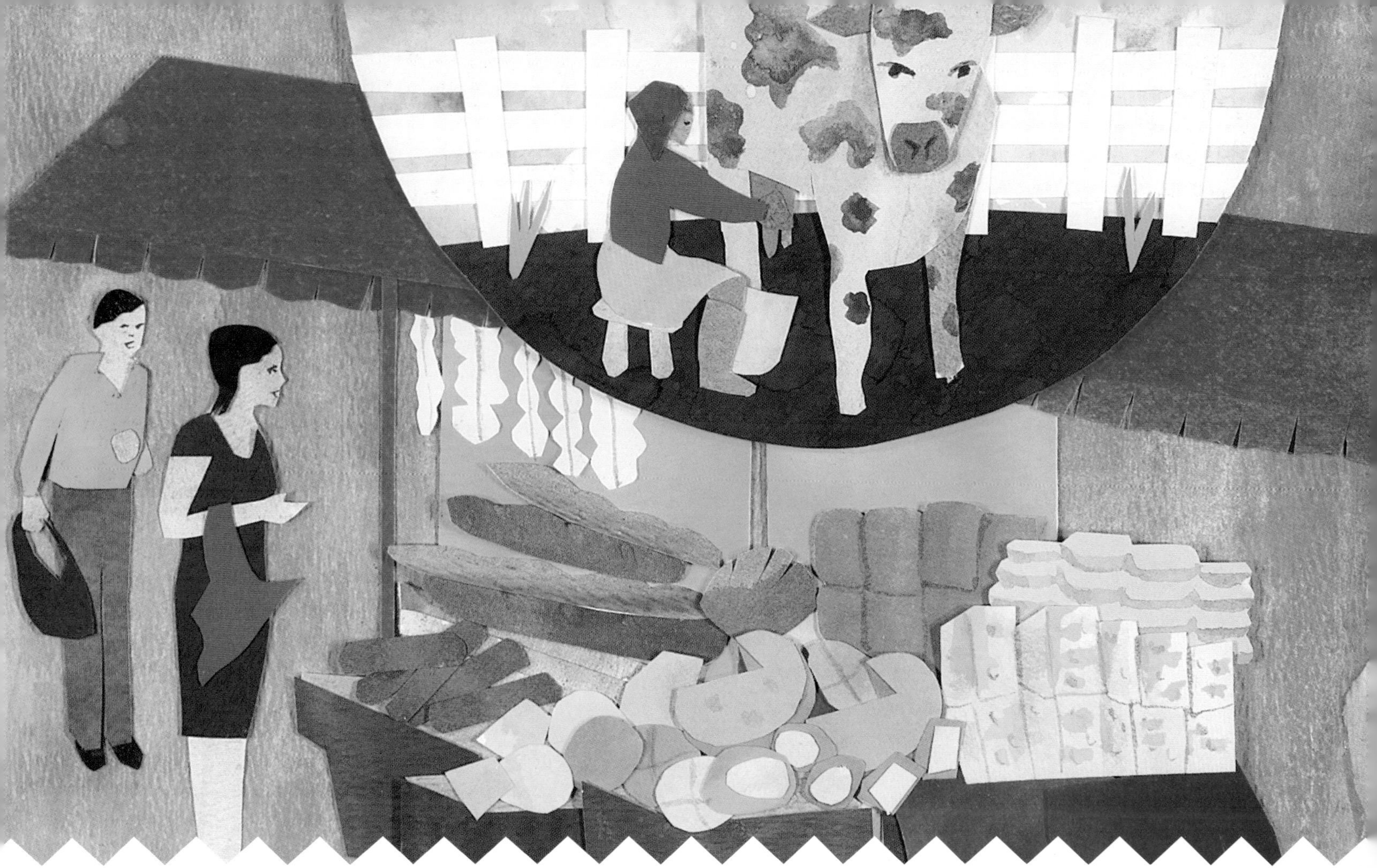

Cheese from France.

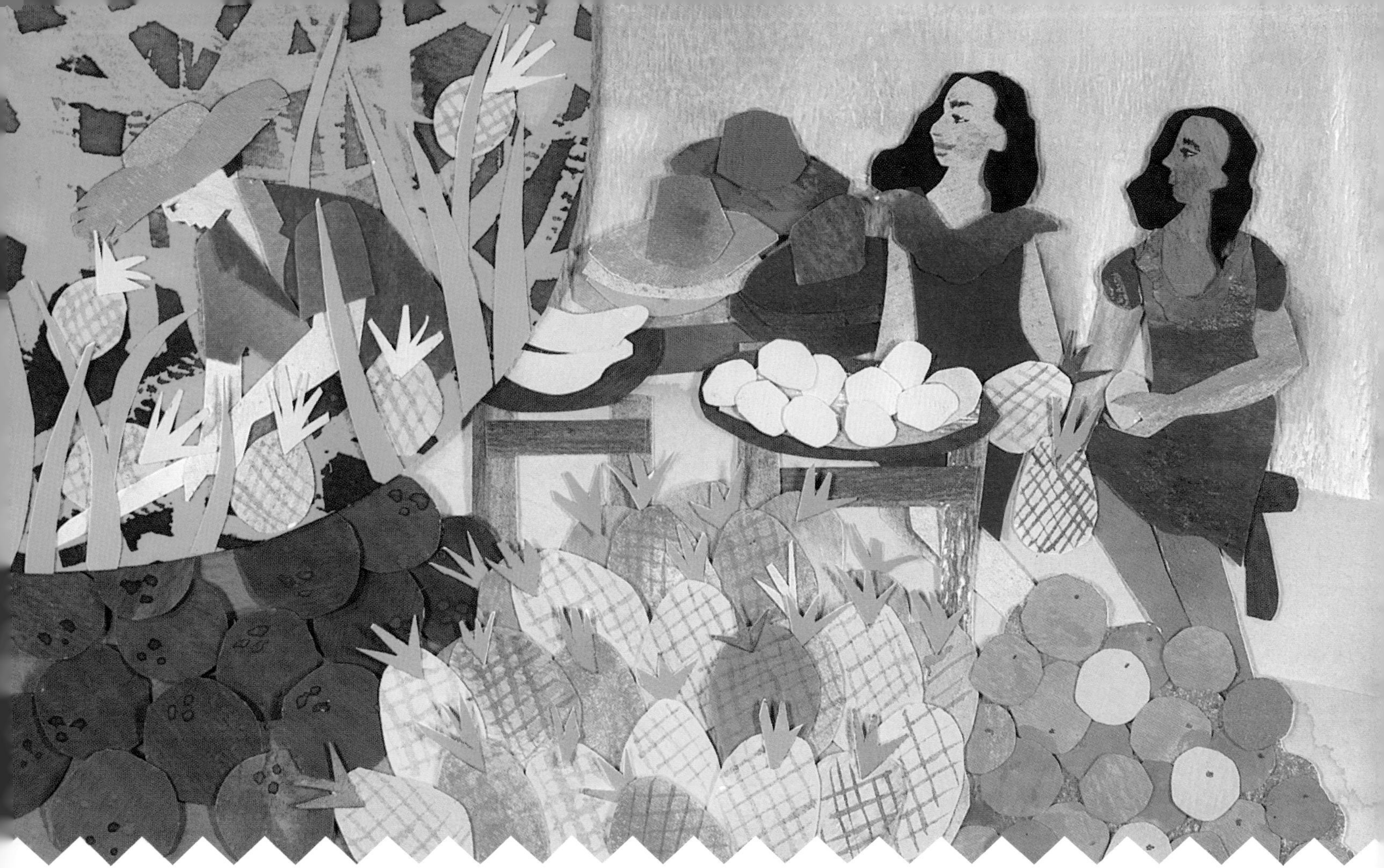

Pineapples from Hawaii.

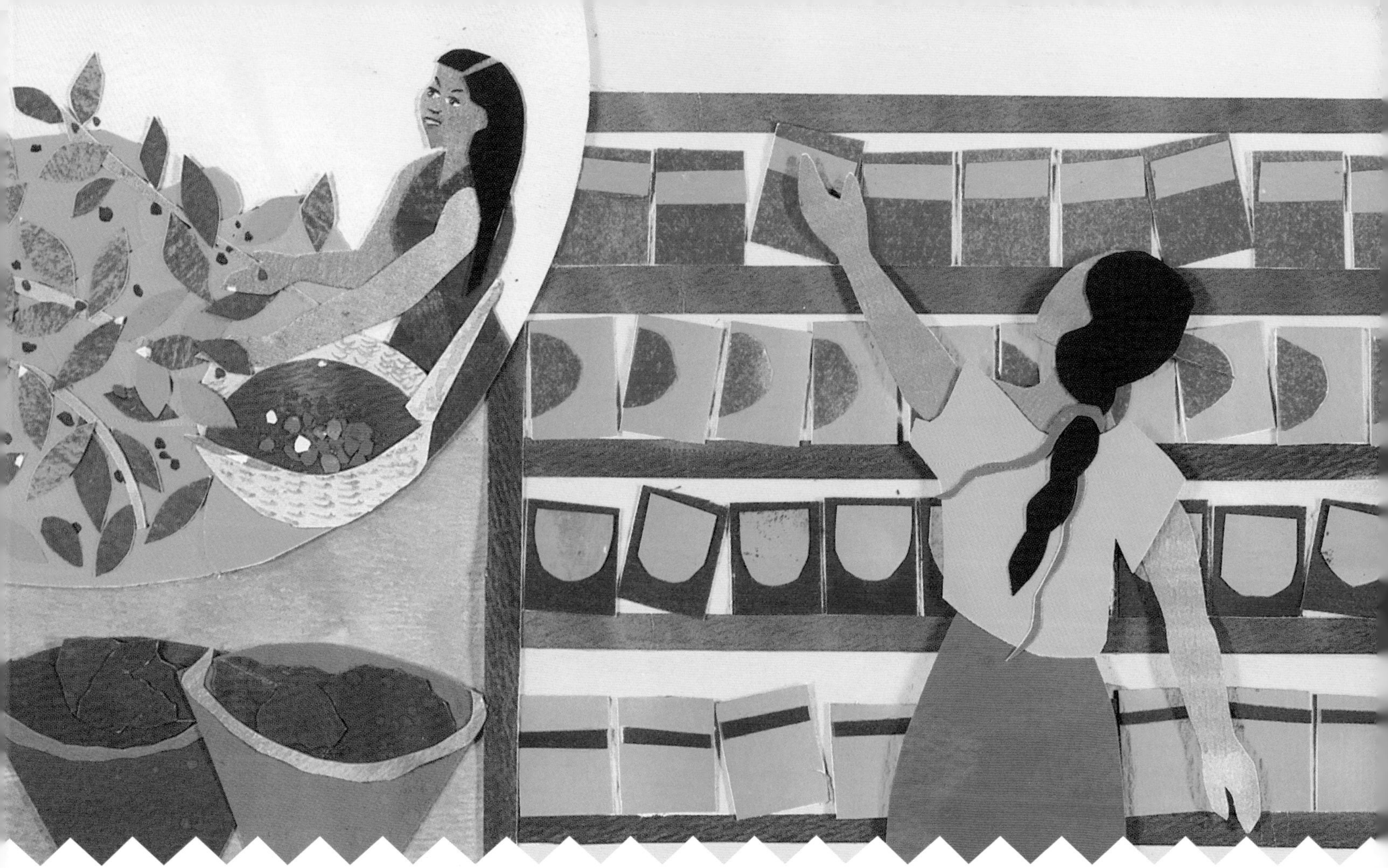

Coffee from Brazil.

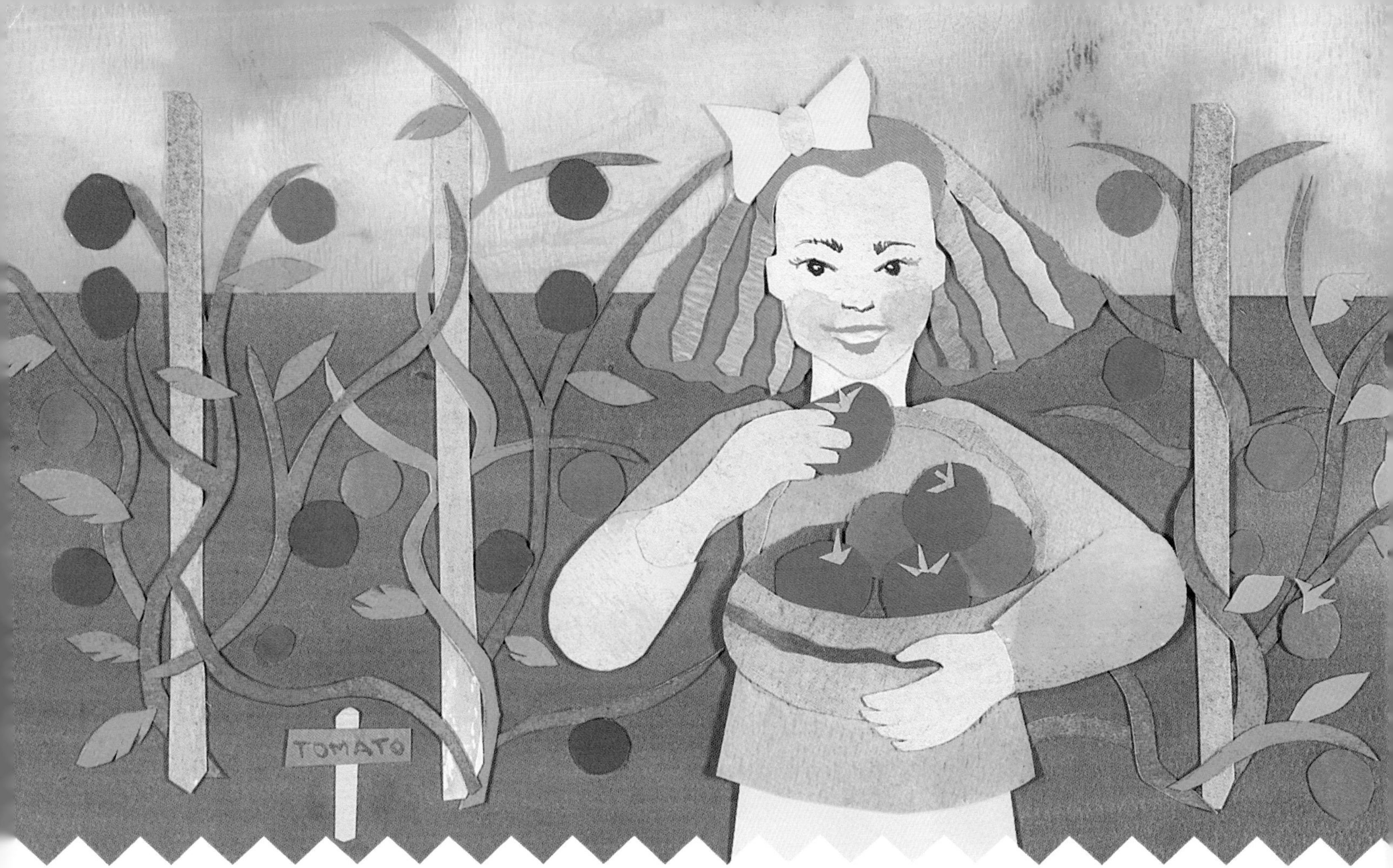

Tomatoes from my very own garden!